# ERIC CLAPTON'S BEST

## CONTENTS

COVER PHOTO BY JEFFERY MAYER

ISBN 978-0-7935-3622-1

HAL•LEONARD®
CORPORATION
7777 W. BLUEMOUND RD. P.O. BOX 13819 MILWAUKEE, WI 53213

# USING THE EASY GUITAR STRUM AND PICK PATTERNS

This chart contains the suggested Strum and Pick Patterns that are referred to by number at the beginning of each song in this book.

The symbols ⊓ and ∨ in the Strum Patterns refer to down and up strokes, respectively.

The letters in the Picking Patterns indicate which right-hand finger plays which string in the pattern:

**p** = thumb
**i** = index finger
**m** = middle finger
**a** = ring finger

For example, Picking Pattern 2 is played:  thumb—index—middle—ring.

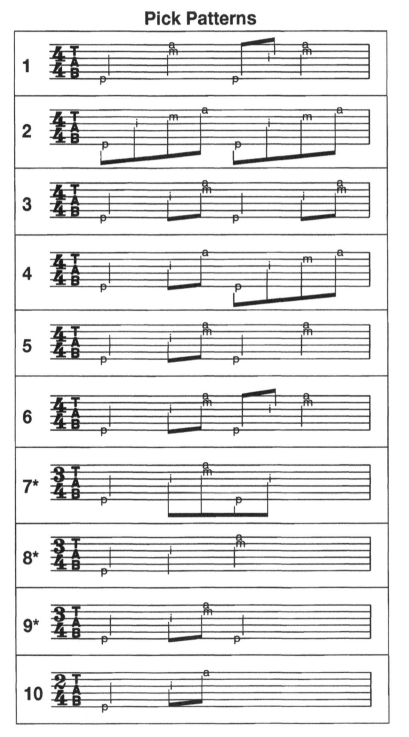

| Strum Patterns | Pick Patterns |
|---|---|

\* You can use the 3/4 Strum or Pick Patterns in songs written in compound meter (6/8, 6/4, 9/8, etc.). Simply play the three-beat pattern two or more times per measure to account for the additonal beats.  For example, you can accompany a song in 6/4 by playing the 3/4 pattern twice in each measure.

# Hideaway

Words and Music by Freddy King and Sonny Thompson

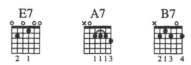

**Strum Pattern: 3**

**Moderate Blues With a Swing Feel** ♩ = 128

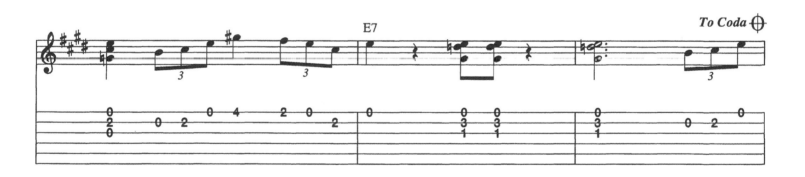

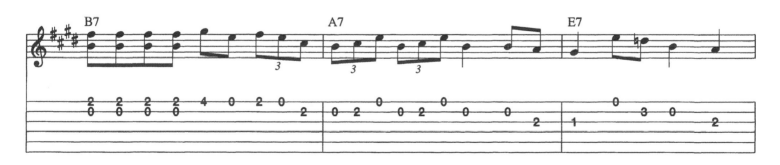

**Rock Beat**

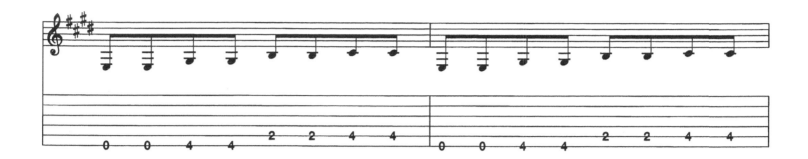

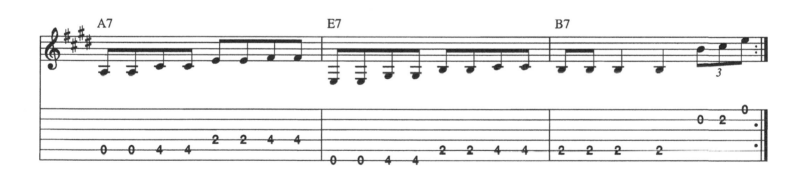

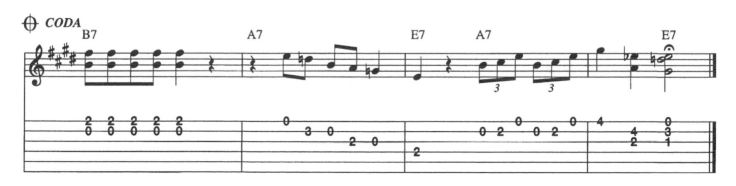

# After Midnight

**Words and Music by John J. Cale**

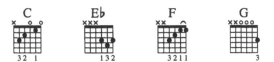

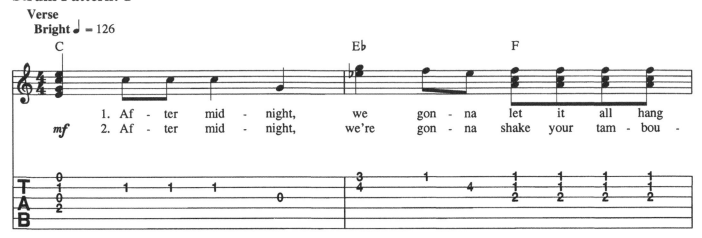

**Strum Pattern: 1**

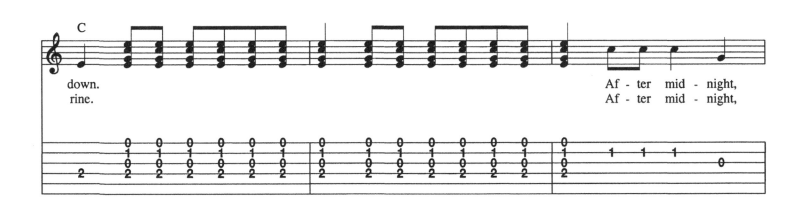

1. Af - ter mid - night, we gon - na let it all hang
2. Af - ter mid - night, we're gon - na shake your tam - bou -

down.
rine.

Af - ter mid - night,
Af - ter mid - night,

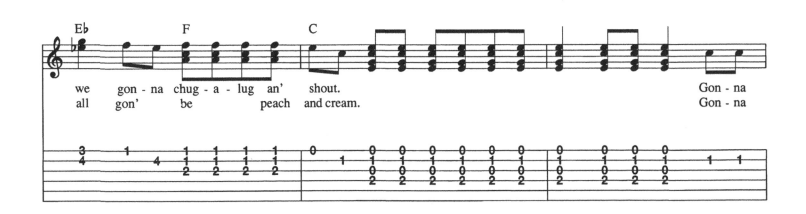

we gon - na chug - a - lug an' shout.
all gon' be peach and cream.

Gon - na
Gon - na

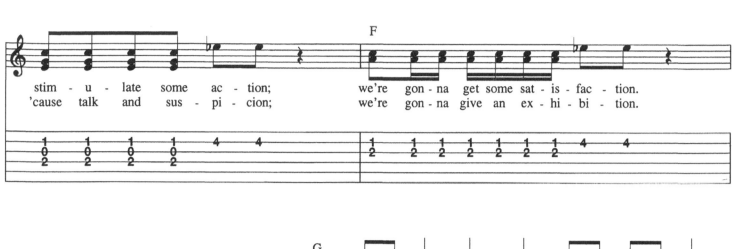

stim - u - late some ac - tion;     we're gon - na get some sat - is - fac - tion.
'cause talk and sus - pi - cion;     we're gon - na give an ex - hi - bi - tion.

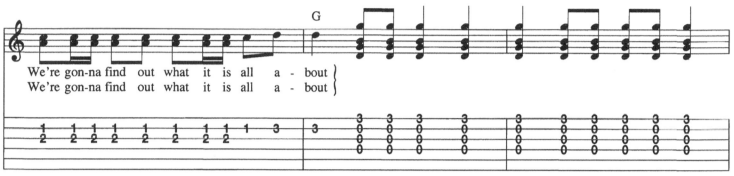

We're gon-na find out what it is all a - bout
We're gon-na find out what it is all a - bout

Af - ter mid - night, we gon - na let it all hang down.

Let me tell you 'bout mid - night.

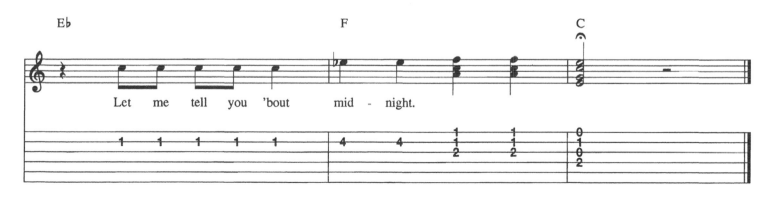

Let me tell you 'bout mid - night.

# Bad Love

**Words and Music by Eric Clapton and Mick Jones**

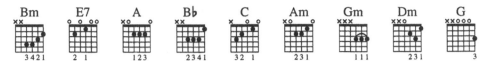

**Strum Pattern: 1**

Verse
Moderately ♩ = 96

1. Oh, what a feel - ing I get when I'm _____ with
2. And now I see _____ that my life has been _____ so

you. _____ You take my heart _ in - to
blue, _____ with all the heart - aches I

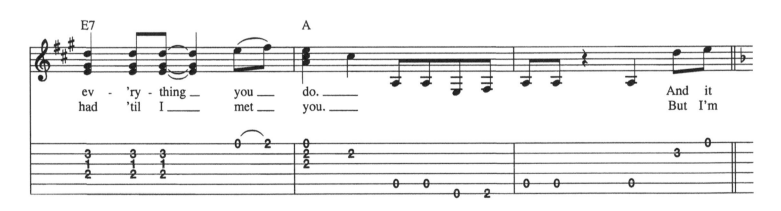

ev - 'ry - thing _ you _ do. _____ And it
had 'til I _____ met _ you. _____ But I'm

**Pre-Chorus**

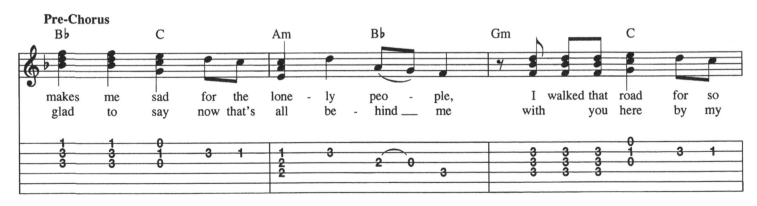

makes me sad for the lone - ly peo - ple, I walked that road for so
glad to say now that's all be - hind _ me with you here by my

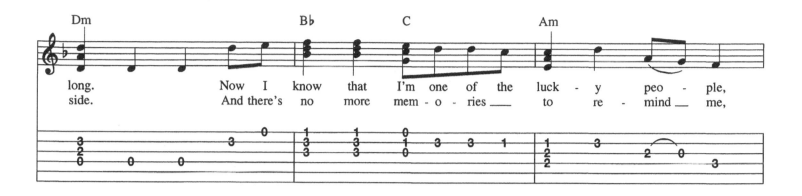

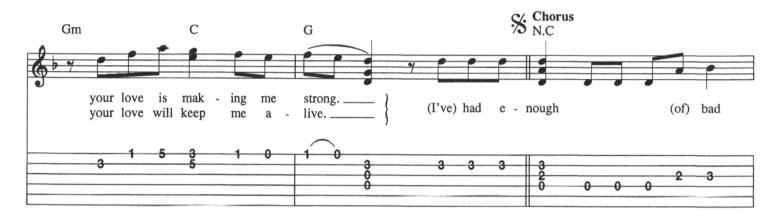

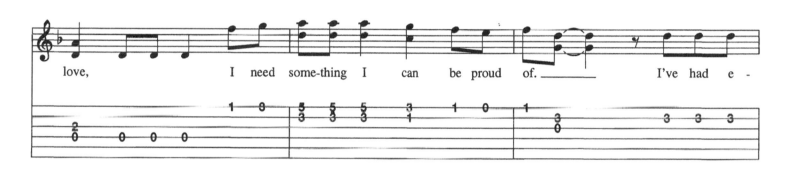

# Badge

### Words and Music by Eric Clapton and George Harrison

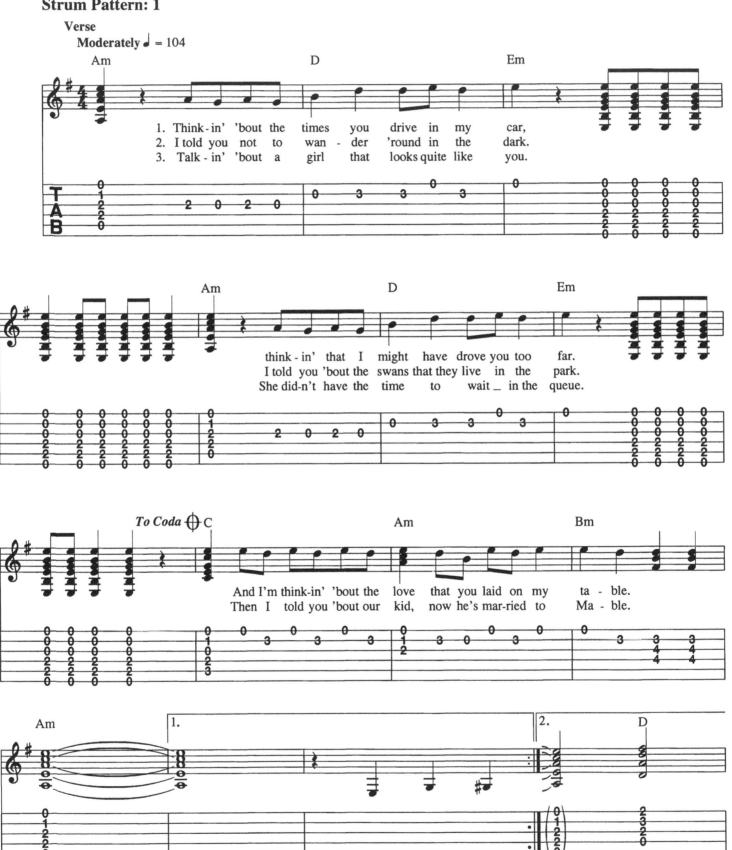

Strum Pattern: 1

Verse
Moderately ♩ = 104

1. Think-in' 'bout the times you drive in my car,
2. I told you not to wan-der 'round in the dark.
3. Talk-in' 'bout a girl that looks quite like you.

think-in' that I might have drove you too far.
I told you 'bout the swans that they live in the park.
She did-n't have the time to wait __ in the queue.

To Coda ⊕ C

And I'm think-in' 'bout the love that you laid on my ta-ble.
Then I told you 'bout our kid, now he's mar-ried to Ma-ble.

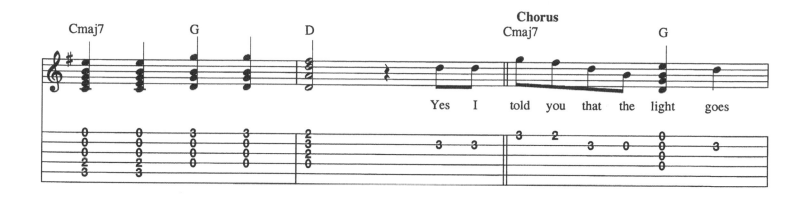

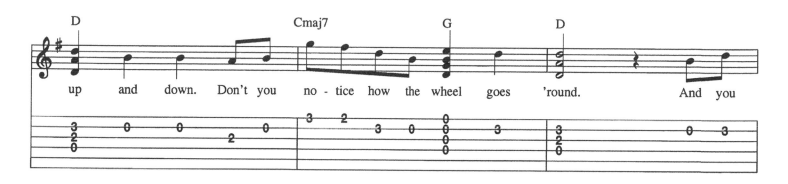

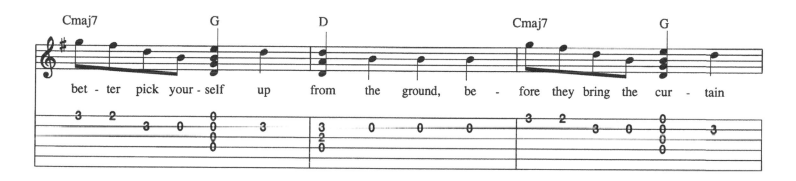

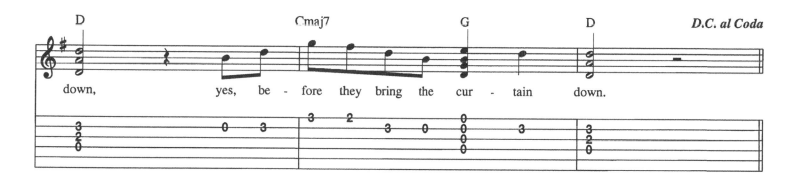

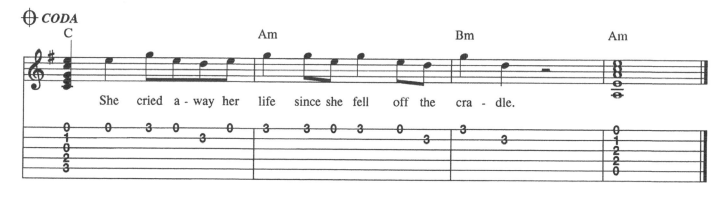

11

# Before You Accuse Me

## (Take A Look At Yourself)

**Words and Music by Eugene McDaniels**

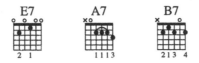

**Strum Pattern: 1**

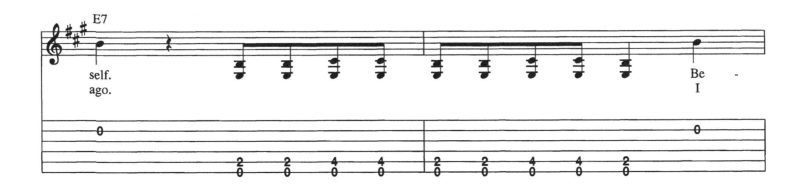

*Additional Lyrics*

3. Before you accuse me, take a look at yourself.
Before you accuse me, take a look at yourself.
You say I'm spendin' money on another women,
(You) been takin' money from someone else.

4. Come on back home baby, try my love one more time.
Come on back home baby, try my love one more time.
You know I don't know when to quit you.
I'm gonna lose my mind.

5. Before you accuse me, take a look at yourself.
Before you accuse me, take a look at yourself.
You say I'm spendin' money on another women,
(You) been takin' money from someone else.

# Cocaine

Words and Music by John J. Cale

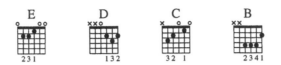

**Strum Pattern: 1**

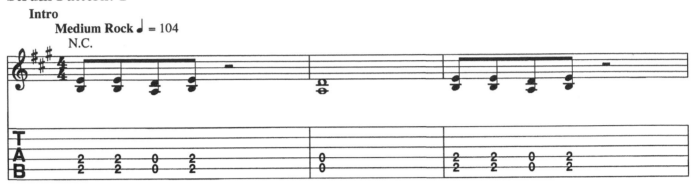

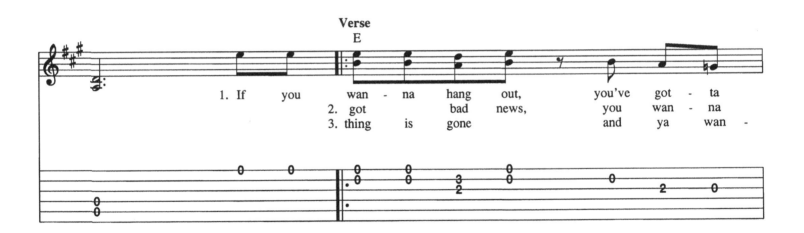

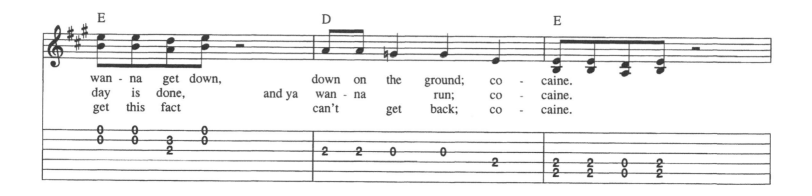

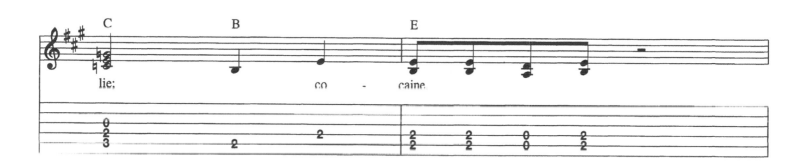

# Crossroads

**Words and Music by Robert Johnson**

**Strum Pattern: 1**

1. I went
2. I went
3.,4. *See Additional Lyrics*

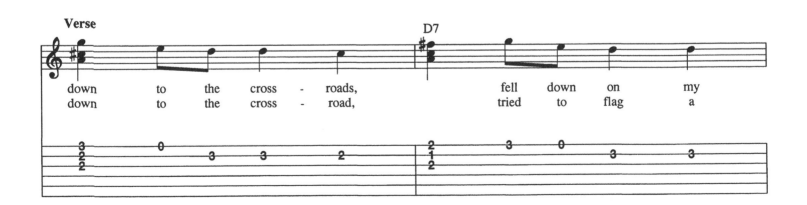

**Verse**

down to the cross - roads, fell down on my
down to the cross - road, tried to flag a

*Additional Lyrics*

3. Well I'm goin' down to Rosedale,
   Take my rider by my side.
   Goin' down to Rosedale,
   Take my rider by my side.
   We can still Barrelhouse baby,
   On the riverside.

4. You can run, you can run,
   Tell my friend, boy, Willie Brown.
   Run, you can run,
   Tell my boyfriend, Willie Brown.
   And I'm standin' at the Crossroad,
   Believe I'm sinkin' down.

# Forever Man

**Words and Music by Jerry Lynn Williams**

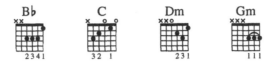

**Strum Pattern: 1**

1. How man - y times must I
2. How man - y times must I

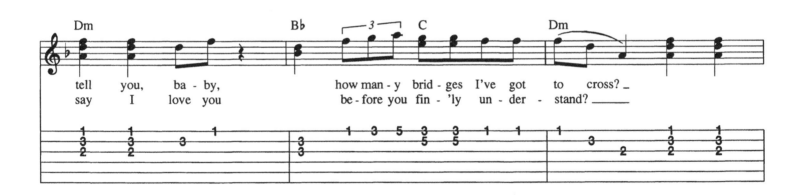

tell you, ba - by, how man - y brid - ges I've got to cross? _
say I love you be - fore you fin - 'ly un - der - stand? _____

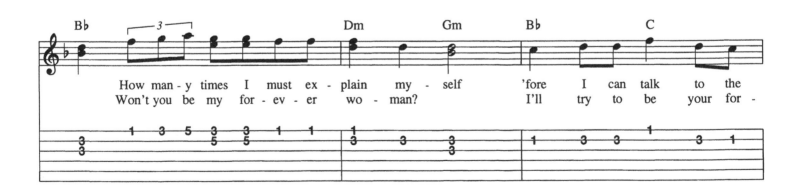

How man - y times I must ex - plain my - self 'fore I can talk to the
Won't you be my for - ev - er wo - man? I'll try to be your for -

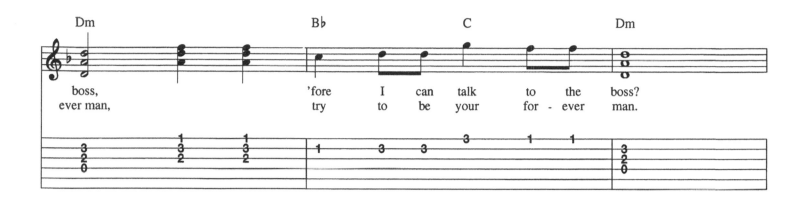

boss,
ever man,

'fore I can talk to the boss?
try to be your for-ever man.

**1.**

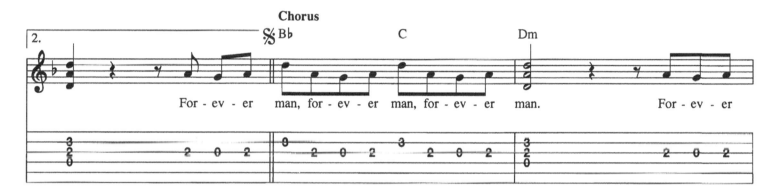

**2.**

**Chorus**

For - ev - er man, for - ev - er man, for - ev - er man.
For - ev - er

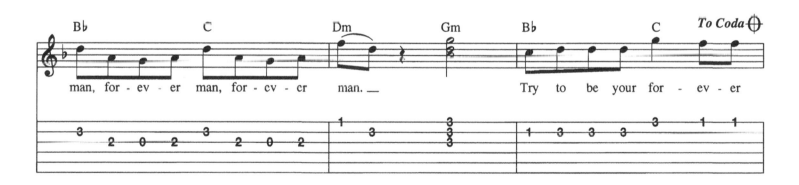

man, for - ev - er man, for - ev - er man. ___

Try to be your for - ev - er

**To Coda** ⊕

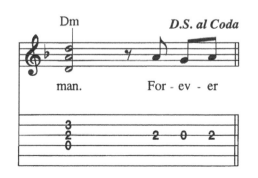

man. For - ev - er

**D.S. al Coda**

⊕ **CODA**

man.

**Repeat and Fade**

# Hard Times

**Words and Music by Ray Charles**

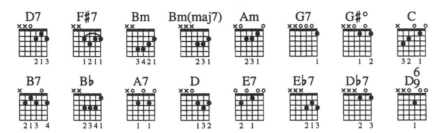

**Strum Pattern: 1**

Slow Blues ♩ = 60

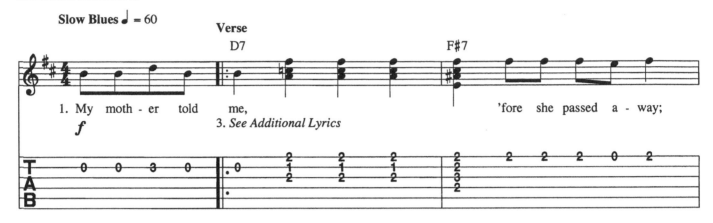

1. My moth-er told me, 'fore she passed a-way;
3. *See Additional Lyrics*

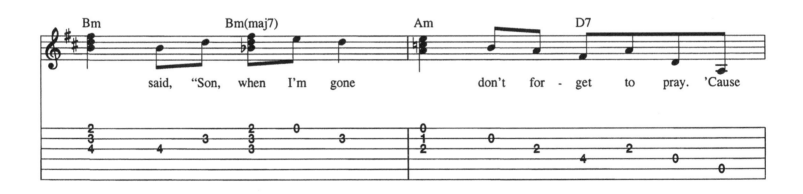

said, "Son, when I'm gone don't for-get to pray. 'Cause

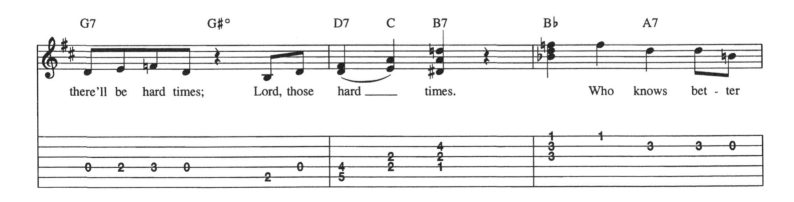

there'll be hard times; Lord, those hard _____ times. Who knows bet-ter

*Additional Lyrics*

3. I had a woman, who was always around,
   But when I lost my money, she put me down.
   Talkin' 'bout hard times; Lord those hard,
   Yeah, yeah, who knows better than I?

4. Lord, one of these days
   There'll be no more sorrow, but when I pass away.
   And no more hard times, no more hard,
   Yeah, yeah, who knows better than I?

# Have You Ever Loved A Woman

**Words and Music by Billy Myles**

**Strum Pattern: 1**

**Verse**

**Slow Blues** ♩ = 60

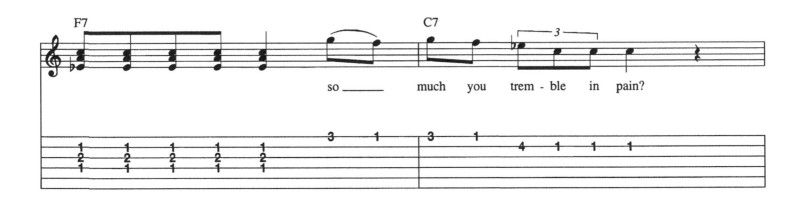

1. Have you ev-er loved a wom-an
2.,3. *See Additional Lyrics*

so _____ much you trem-ble in pain?

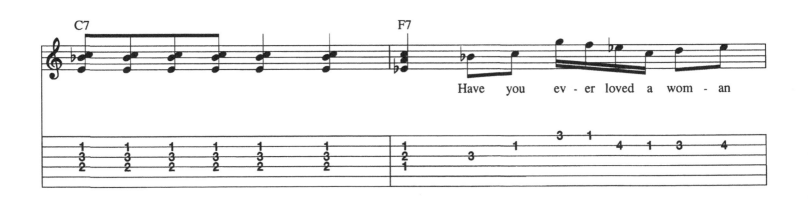

Have you ev-er loved a wom-an

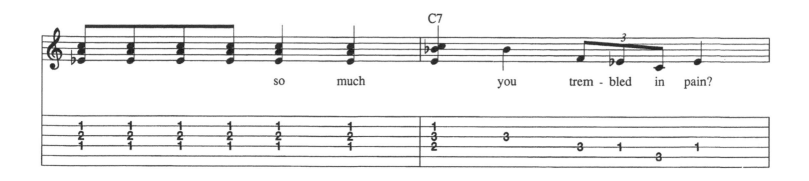

so much you trem - bled in pain?

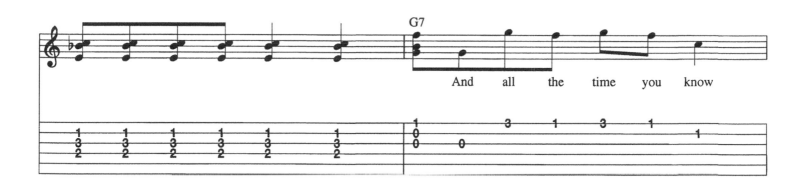

And all the time you know

she bears an - oth - er man's name.

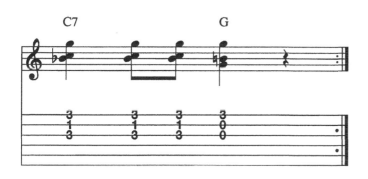

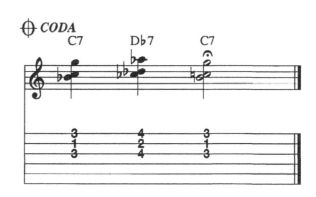

*Additional Lyrics*

2. But you love that woman, so much
   It's a shame and a sin.
   You just love that woman, so much
   It's a shame and a sin.
   But all the time you know, yes you know.
   She belongs to your very best friend.

3. Have you ever loved a woman,
   And you know you can't leave her alone?
   Have you ever loved a woman,
   Yes, and you know you can't leave her alone?
   Something deep inside of you,
   Won't let you wreck your best friend's home.

# I Ain't Got You

## By Calvin Carter

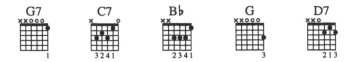

**Strum Pattern: 4**

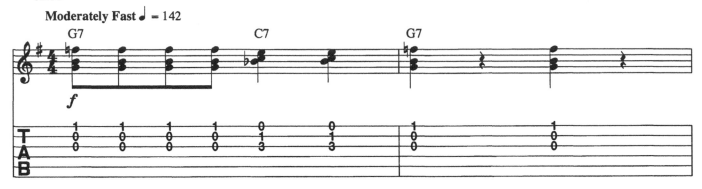

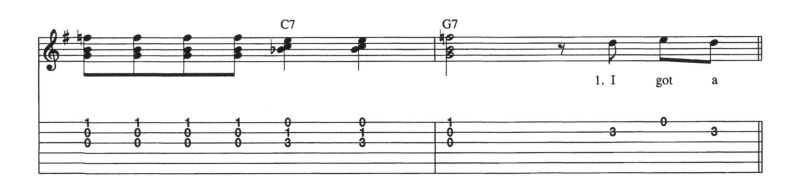

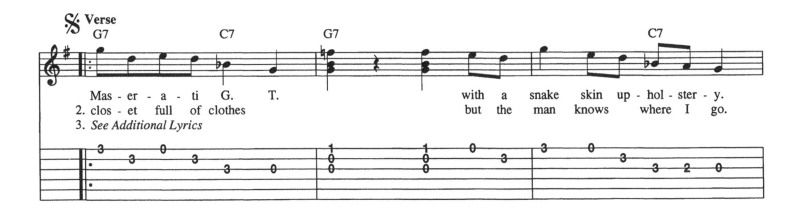

I got a charge ac-count at Gold Blatt's but I
He keeps a ring in my nose. But I

ain't got you.
ain't got you. 2. Got-ta I got a

tav-ern and a li-quor store. I play the num-bers yeah,

four for-ty four. I got a mo-jo. Yeah. Don't you know, I'm

all dressed up but no place to go. 3. I got-ta

*Additional Lyrics*

3. I gotta women to the right of me.
   I gotta women to the left of me.
   I gotta women all around me.
   But I ain't got you.

# I Can't Stand It

**Words and Music by Eric Clapton**

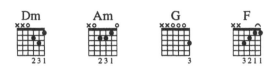

**Strum Pattern: 1**

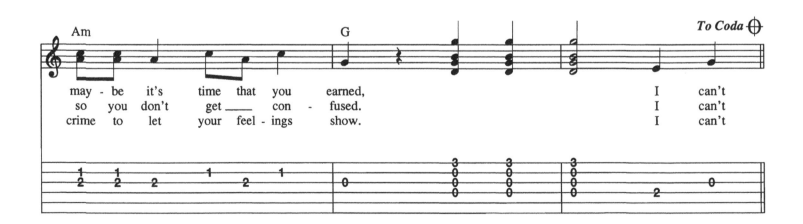

# I Feel Free

Words and Music by Jack Bruce and Pete Brown

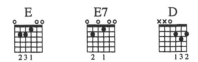

**Strum Pattern: 1**

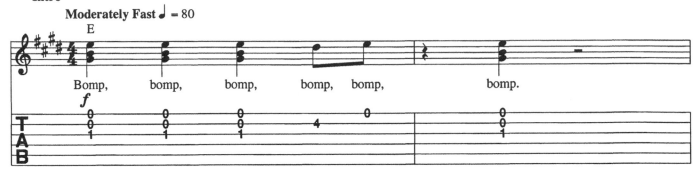

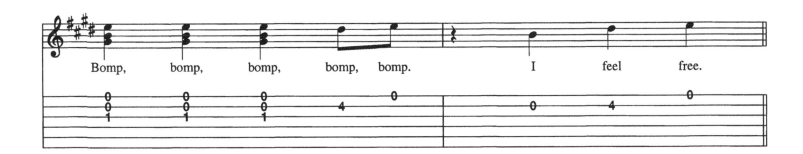

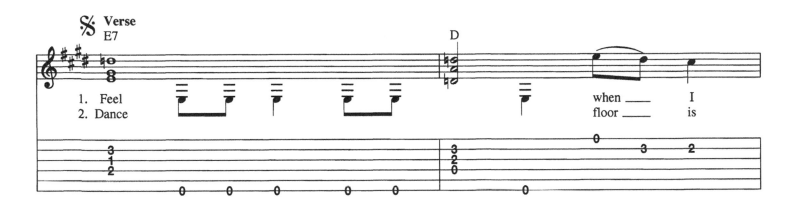

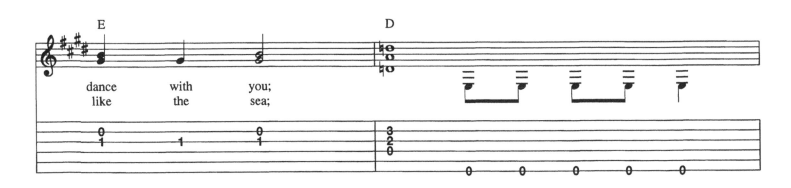

**Bridge**

walk    down    the    street;    there's    no    one    there,    though    the

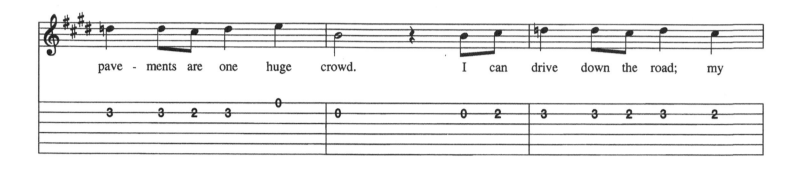

pave - ments    are    one    huge    crowd.    I    can    drive    down    the    road;    my

*D.S. al Coda*

eyes    don't    see,    though    my    mind    wants    to    cry    out    loud.

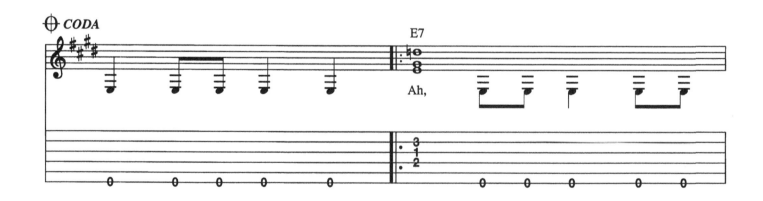

*CODA*

E7

Ah,

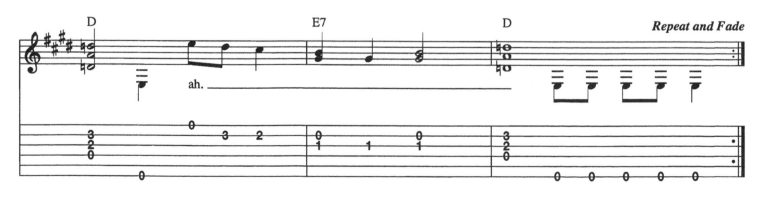

D                                    E7                    D                    *Repeat and Fade*

ah.

30

# Pretending

### Words and Music by Jerry Williams

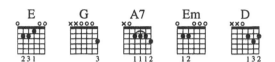

**Strum Pattern: 1**

**Verse**

**Moderately** ♩ = 92

1. How man - y times must we tell the tale?

How man - y times must we fall? Liv - ing in a

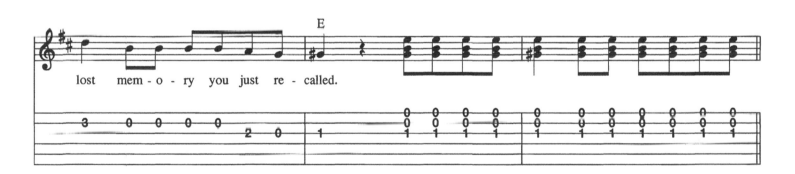

lost mem - o - ry you just re - called.

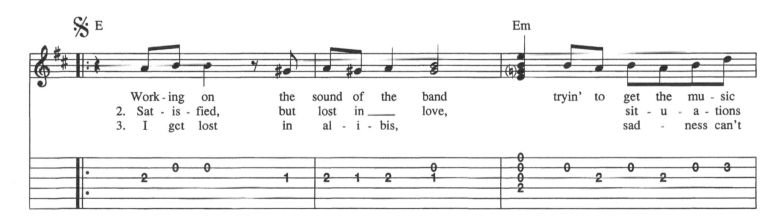

Work - ing on the sound of the band tryin' to get the mu - sic
2. Sat - is - fied, but lost in _____ love, sit - u - a - tions
3. I get lost in al - i - bis, sad - ness can't

right.
change.
pre-vail.

Two go out work - ing, three stay

You're nev - er who you used to think you are, how

Ev - 'ry - bod - y knows strong love can't

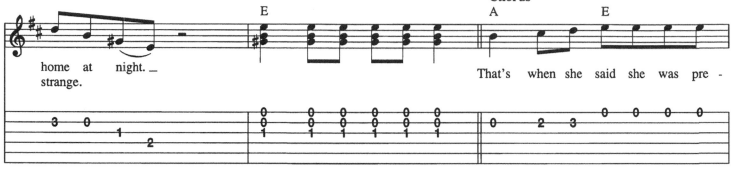

home at night. ___
strange.

**Chorus**

That's when she said she was pre -

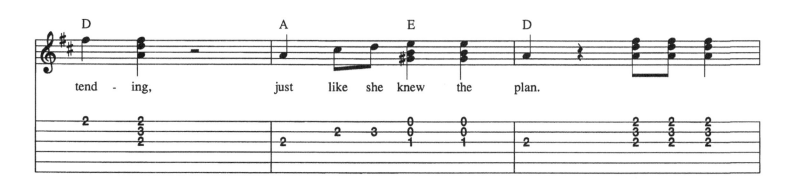

tend - ing,   just like she knew the plan.

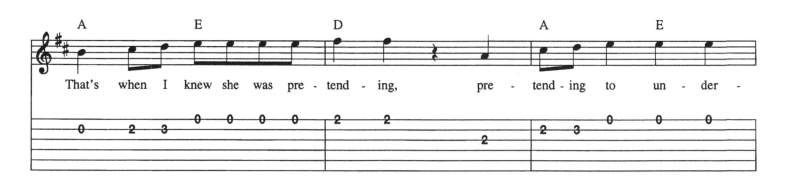

That's when I knew she was pre - tend - ing,   pre - tend - ing to un - der -

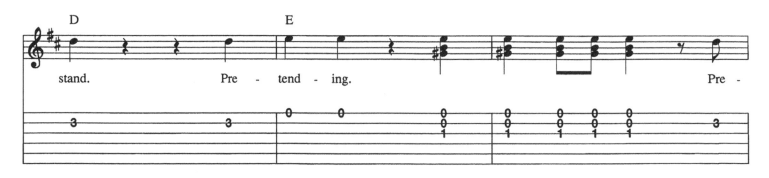

stand.   Pre - tend - ing.   Pre -

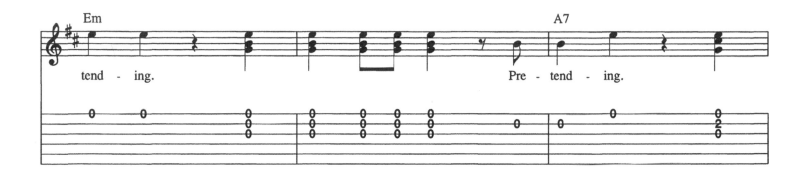

tend - ing. Pre - tend - ing.

*2nd Time*
*D.S. al Coda*

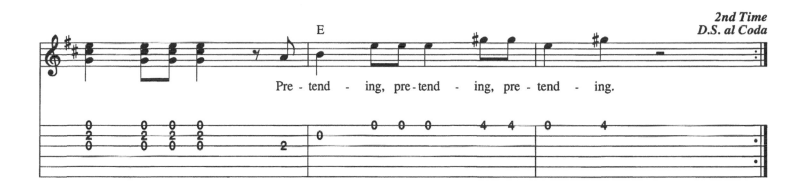

Pre - tend - ing, pre - tend - ing, pre - tend - ing.

CODA

N.C.

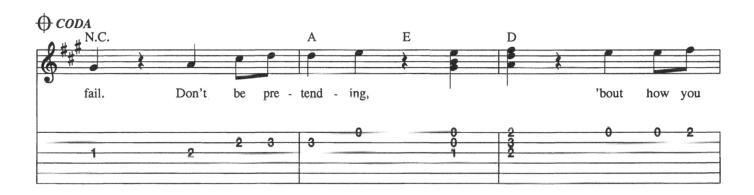

fail. Don't be pre - tend - ing, 'bout how you

feel. Don't be pre - tend - ing,

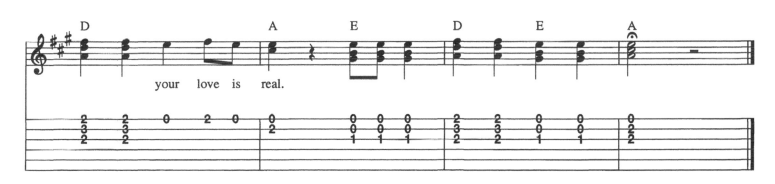

your love is real.

# I Shot The Sheriff

**Words and Music by Bob Marley**

**Strum Pattern: 3**

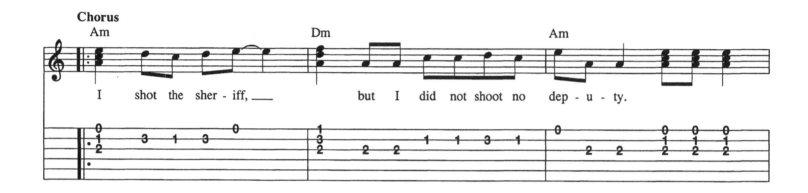

**Chorus**

I shot the sher-iff, ___ but I did not shoot no dep-u-ty.

I shot the sher-iff, ___ but I did not shoot no

dep - u - ty.

**Verse**

1. All a-round in my home-town they're try-ing to track me down.
2.,3.,4. *See Additional Lyrics*

They say they want to bring me in guilt-y

kil-lin' of a dep-u-ty, for

the life of a dep-u-ty. But I say:

*Additional Lyrics*

2. Sheriff John Brown always hated me;
   For what, I don't know.
   And every time that I plant a seed,
   He said, "Kill it before it grows,"
   "Kill it before it grows."

3. Freedom came our way one day,
   So I started out of town.
   All of a sudden, I see Sheriff Brown
   Aimin' to shoot me down,
   So I shot him down.

4. Reflexes got the better of me,
   What will be will be.
   Every day, the bucket goes to the well,
   One day the bottom will drop out
   I say, one day the bottom will drop out.

# Lay Down Sally

Words and Music by Eric Clapton, Marcy Levy and George Terry

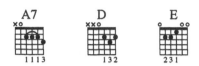

**Strum Pattern: 1**

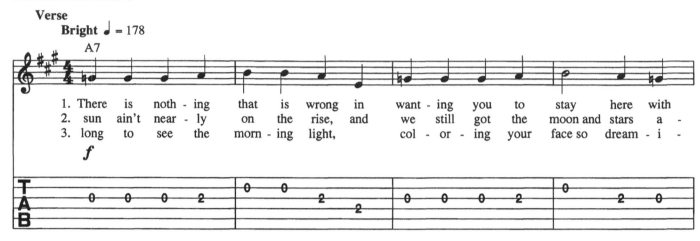

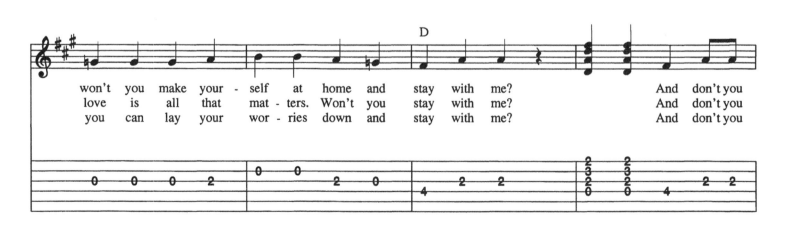

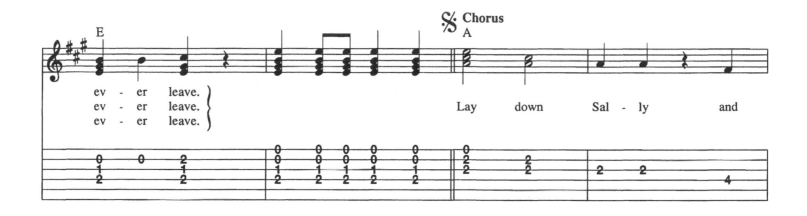

Chorus

ev - er leave.
ev - er leave.
ev - er leave.

Lay down Sal - ly and

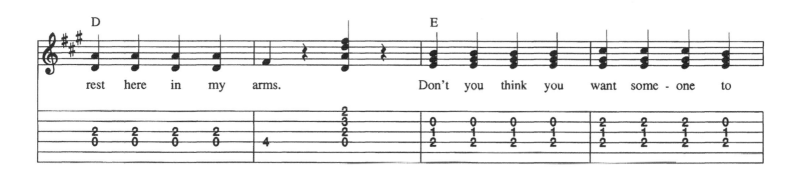

rest here in my arms. Don't you think you want some - one to

talk to? Lay down Sal - ly. No

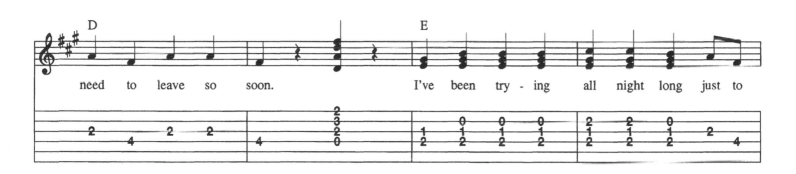

need to leave so soon. I've been try - ing all night long just to

talk to you.

2. The talk to you.

3. I

D.S. and Fade

37

# Layla

**Words and Music by Eric Clapton and Jim Gordon**

**Strum Pattern: 3**
**Pick Pattern: 3**

**Intro**

Moderately Slow ♩ = 92

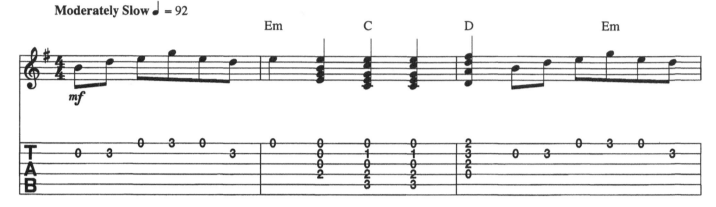

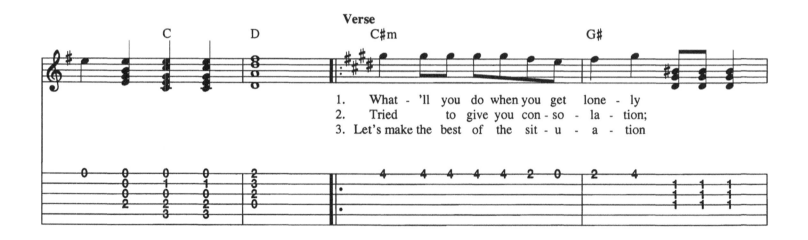

1. What - 'll you do when you get lone - ly
2. Tried to give you con - so - la - tion;
3. Let's make the best of the sit - u - a - tion

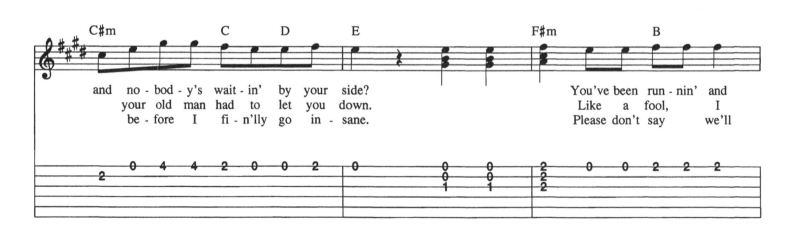

and no - bod - y's wait - in' by your side?
your old man had to let you down.
be - fore I fi - n'lly go in - sane.

You've been run - nin' and
Like a fool, I
Please don't say we'll

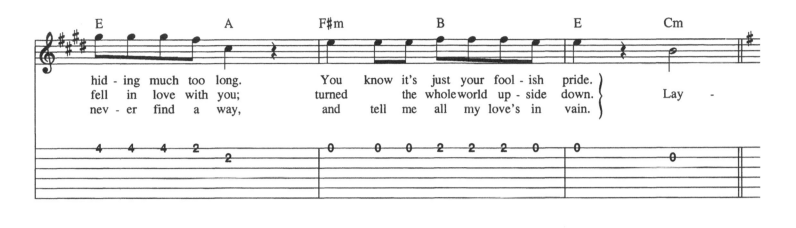

hid - ing much too long.   You know it's just your fool - ish pride.
fell in love with you;   turned the whole world up - side down.   } Lay -
nev - er find a way,   and tell me all my love's in vain.

**Chorus**

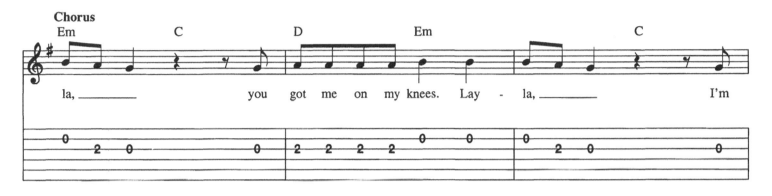

la, _____ you got me on my knees. Lay - la, _____ I'm

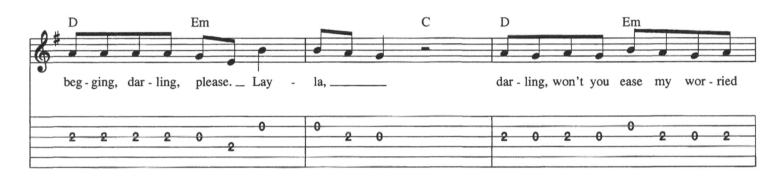

beg - ging, dar - ling, please. ___ Lay - la, _____ dar - ling, won't you ease my wor - ried

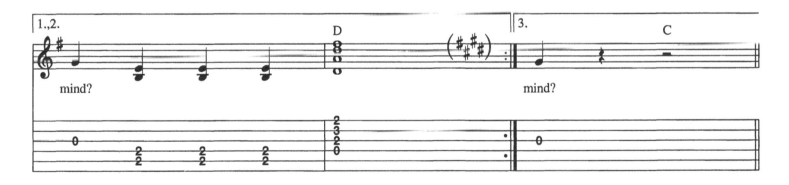

mind?                                                                     mind?

*Repeat and Fade*

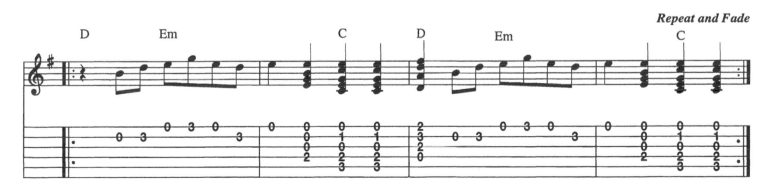

# Let It Grow

**Words and Music by Eric Clapton**

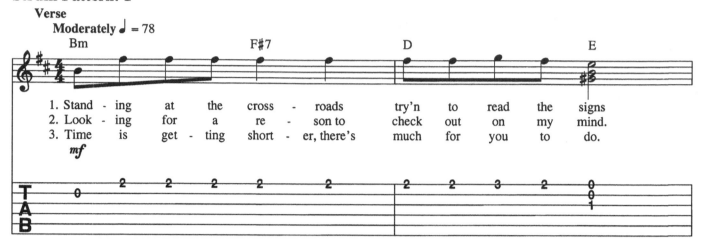

**Strum Pattern: 1**

**Verse**
**Moderately** ♩ = 78

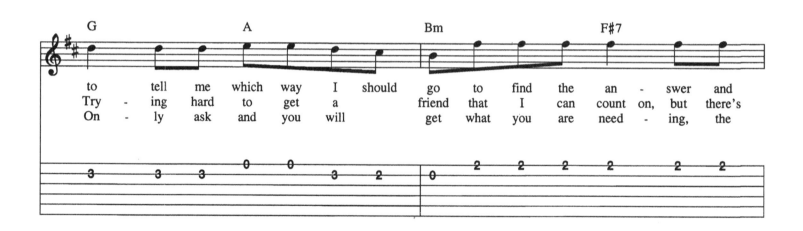

1. Stand - ing    at    the    cross - roads    try'n    to    read    the    signs
2. Look - ing    for    a    re - son to    check    out    on    my    mind.
3. Time    is    get - ting    short - er, there's    much    for    you    to    do.

*mf*

to    tell    me    which    way    I    should    go    to    find    the    an - swer    and
Try - ing    hard    to    get    a    friend    that    I    can    count    on,    but    there's
On - ly    ask    and    you    will    get    what    you    are    need - ing,    the

all    the    time    I    know.
noth - ing    left    to    show.
rest    is    up    to    you.

Plant    your    love    and    let    it    grow.

**Chorus**

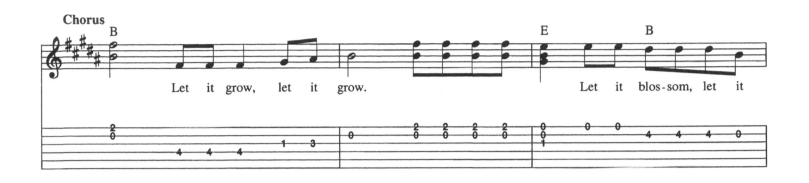

Let it grow, let it grow. Let it blos-som, let it

flow. In the sun, the rain, the snow.

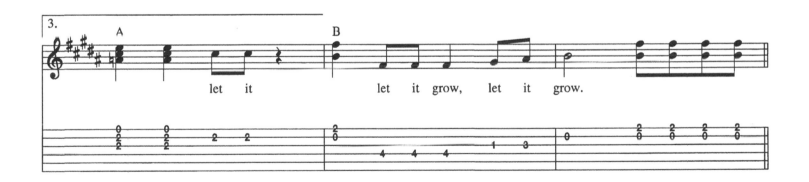

Love is love - ly, let it grow.

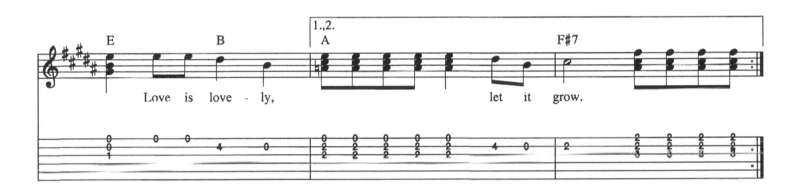

let it let it grow, let it grow.

*Repeat and Fade*

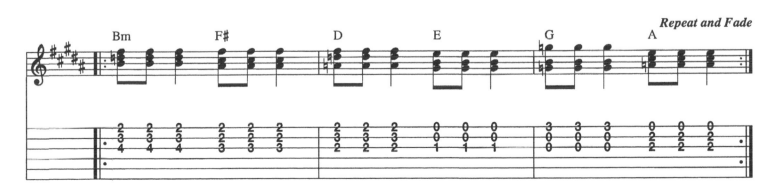

# Ramblin' On My Mind

**Words and Music by Robert Johnson**

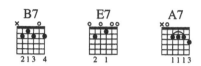

**Strum Pattern: 1**

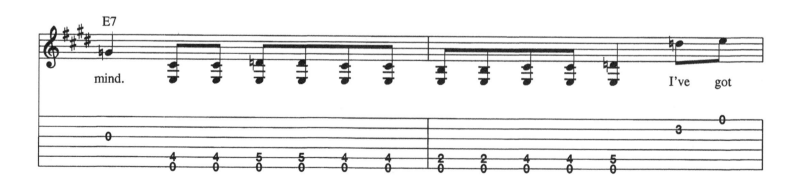

ram - blin' I've got ram-blin' all on my

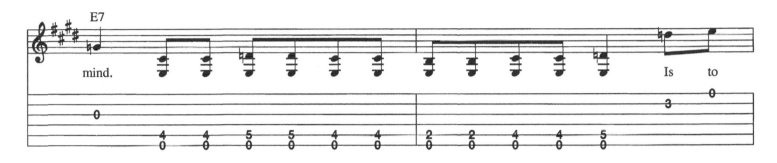

mind. Is to

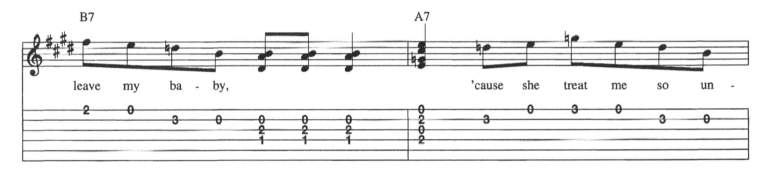

leave my ba - by, 'cause she treat me so un -

kind. _____ 2. I'm goin'

*Additional Lyrics*

2. I'm goin' down to the station,
   Catch the fastest train I see.
   I'm goin' down to the station,
   Catch the fastest train I see.
   I got the blues about her sold soul,
   And the sun got the blues 'bout me.

3. I got neat things,
   I got neat things all on my mind.
   Little girl, little girl,
   I got neat things all on my mind.
   Is to leave my baby,
   'Cause she treats me so unkind.

# Strange Brew

Words and Music by Eric Clapton, Felix Pappalardi and Gail Collins

**Strum Pattern: 1**

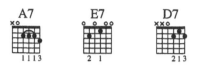

**Verse**

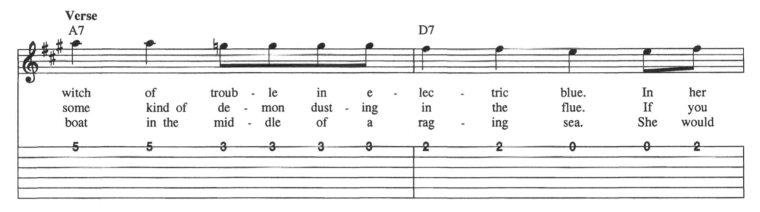

witch of troub - le in e - lec - tric blue. In her
some kind of de - mon dust - ing in the flue. If her you
boat in the mid - dle of a rag - ing sea. She would

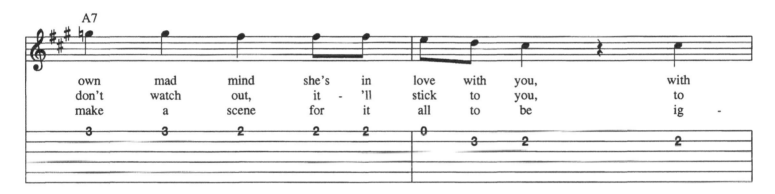

own mad mind she's in love with you, with
don't watch out, it - 'll stick to you, to
make a scene for it all to be ig -

you. Now what you gon - na
you. What kind of fool are
nored. And would - n't you be

do?
you?
bored?

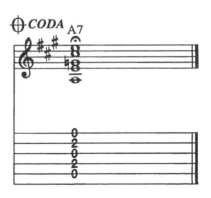

# Tulsa Time

**Words and Music by Danny Flowers**

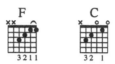

**Strum Pattern: 4**

**Intro**

**Moderate Country** ♩ = 120

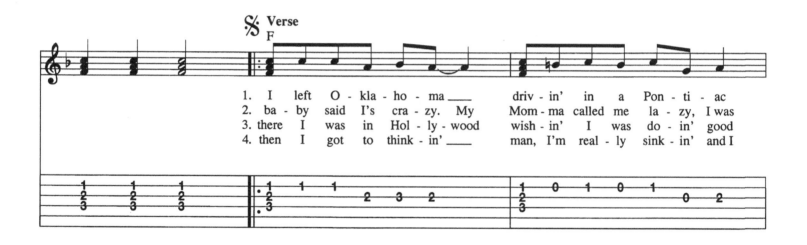

1. I left O - kla - ho - ma ___ driv - in' in a Pon - ti - ac
2. ba - by said I's cra - zy. My Mom - ma called me la - zy, I was
3. there I was in Hol - ly - wood wish - in' I was do - in' good
4. then I got to think - in' ___ man, I'm real - ly sink - in' and I

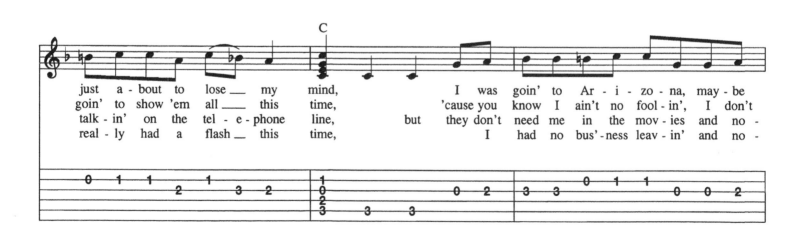

just a - bout to lose ___ my mind, I was goin' to Ar - i - zo - na, may - be
goin' to show 'em all ___ this time, 'cause you know I ain't no fool - in', I don't
talk - in' on the tel - e - phone line, but they don't need me in the mov - ies and no -
real - ly had a flash ___ this time, I had no bus' - ness leav - in' and no -

on to Cal - i - for - nia where the peo - ple all ___ live ___ so fine.  My
need no more school - in' I was guess I'm just a waist - in' time.  Well,
bod - y sings my songs,
bod - y would be griev - in' if I

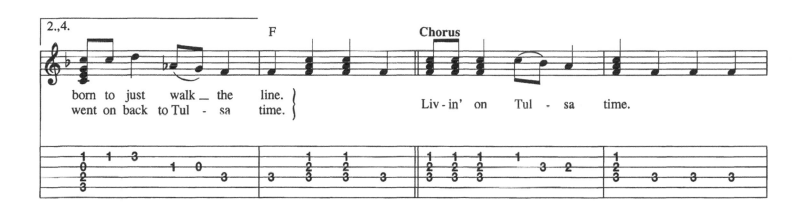

born to just walk ___ the line.
went on back to Tul - sa time.

**Chorus**

Liv - in' on Tul - sa time.

Liv - in' on Tul - sa time.

Well, you know I been thru it when I
Gon - na set my watch back to it, 'cause you

set my watchback to it,
know I've been thru it,

Liv - in' on Tul - sa time.  Well, time.

# The Sunshine Of Your Love

Words and Music by Jack Bruce, Pete Brown and Eric Clapton

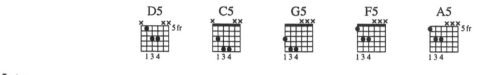

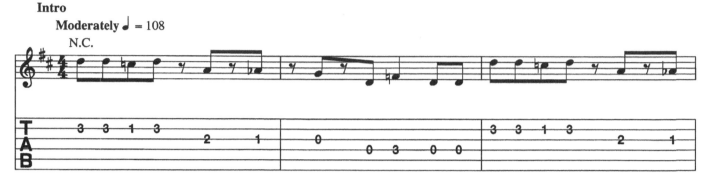

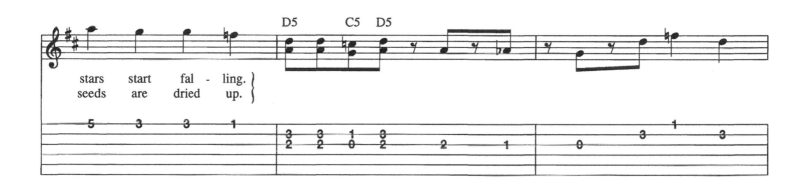

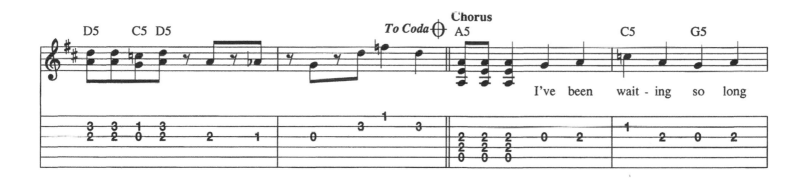

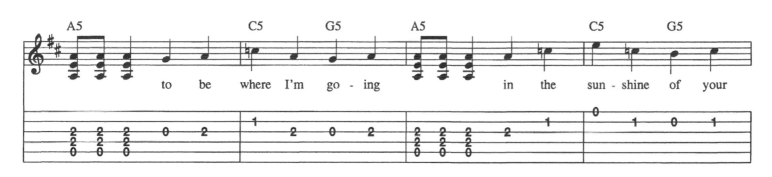

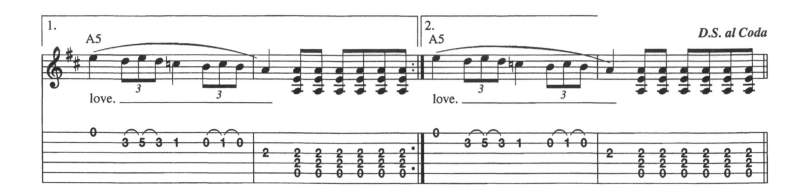

love. love.

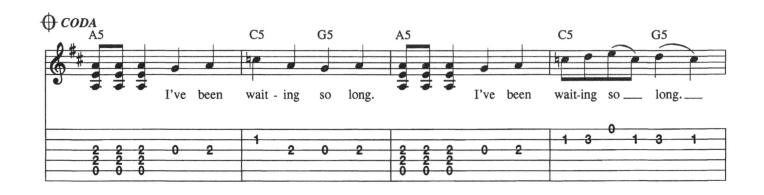

CODA

I've been wait-ing so long. I've been wait-ing so ___ long. ___

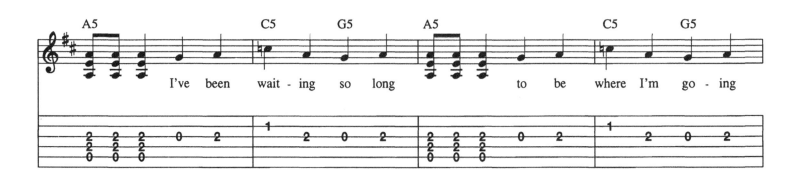

I've been wait-ing so long to be where I'm go-ing

in the sun-shine of your love. ___

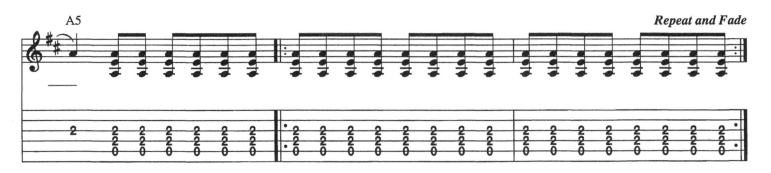

# White Room

### Words and Music by Jack Bruce and Pete Brown

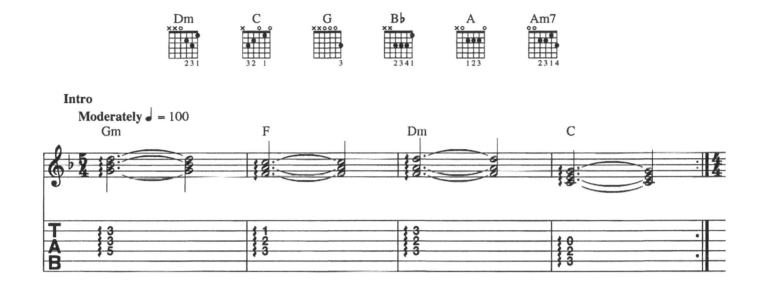

**Intro**
**Moderately** ♩ = 100

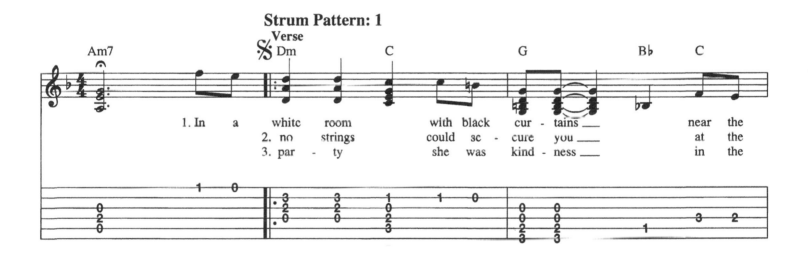

**Strum Pattern: 1**

**Verse**

1. In a white room with black cur- tains ___ near the
2. no strings could se- cure you ___ at the
3. par- ty she was kind- ness ___ in the

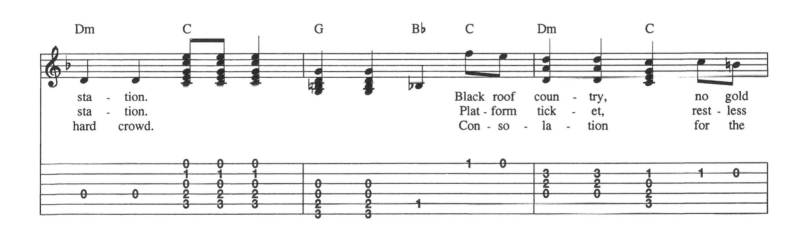

sta- tion.
sta- tion.
hard crowd.

Black roof coun- try, no gold
Plat- form tick- et, rest- less
Con- so- la- tion for the

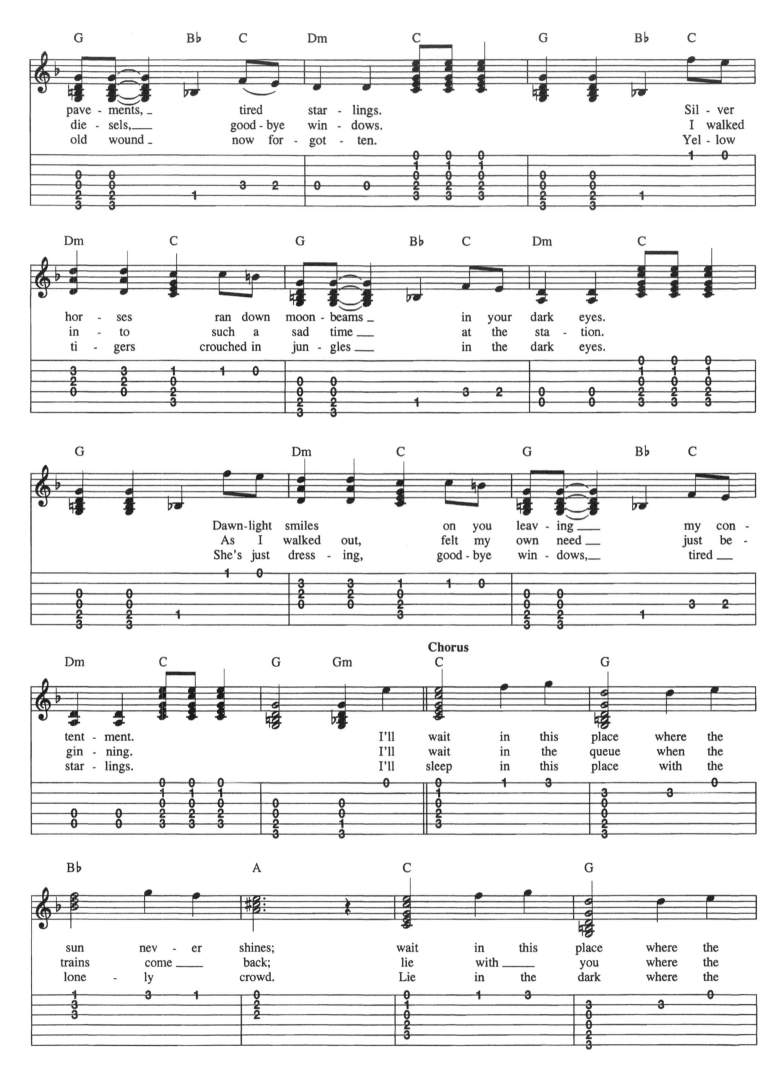

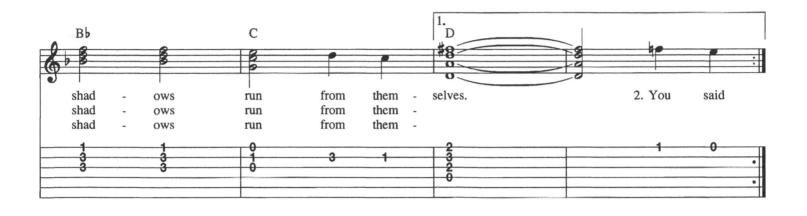

shad - ows run from them - selves.
shad - ows run from them -
shad - ows run from them -

2. You said

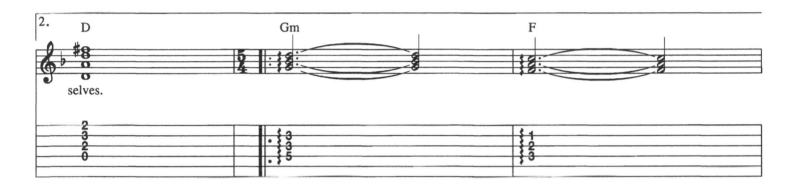

selves.

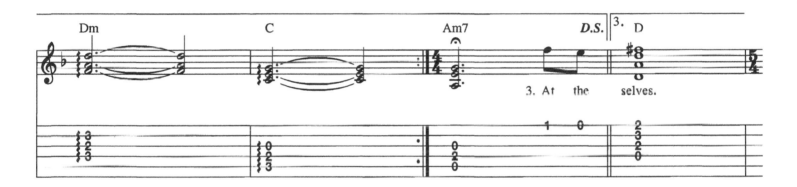

3. At the selves.

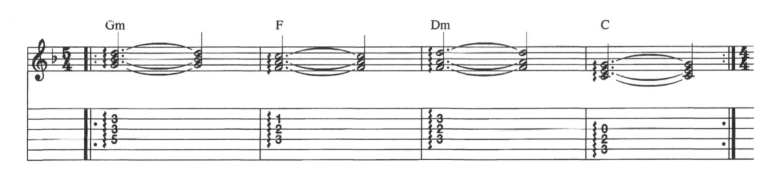

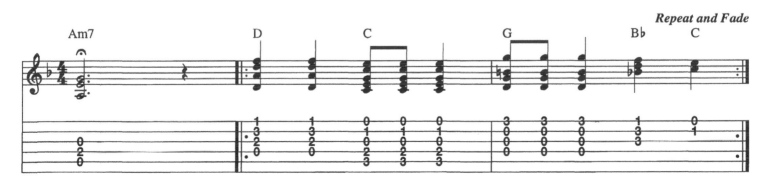

*Repeat and Fade*

# Wonderful Tonight

**Words and Music by Eric Clapton**

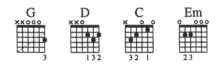

**Strum Pattern: 1**

**Verse**

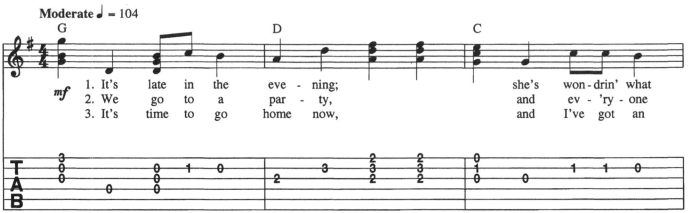

Moderate ♩ = 104

1. It's late in the eve-ning; she's won-drin' what
2. We go to a par-ty, and ev-'ry-one
3. It's time to go home now, and I've got an

clothes to wear. She puts on her make-up
turns to see. This beau-ti-ful la-dy
ach-ing head. So I give her the car keys

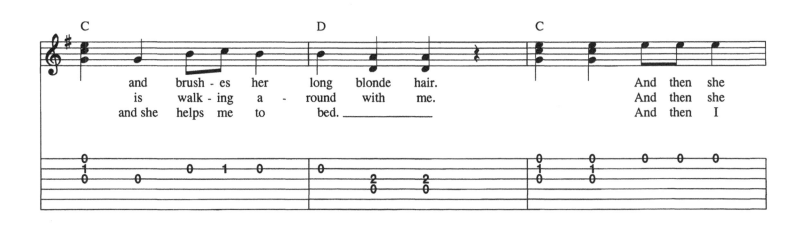

and brush-es her long blonde hair. And then she
is walk-ing a-round with me. And then she
and she helps me to bed. _____ And then I

asks me, "Do I look all right?" and I say,
asks me, "Do you feel all right?" and I say,
tell her, as I turn out the light, I say "My

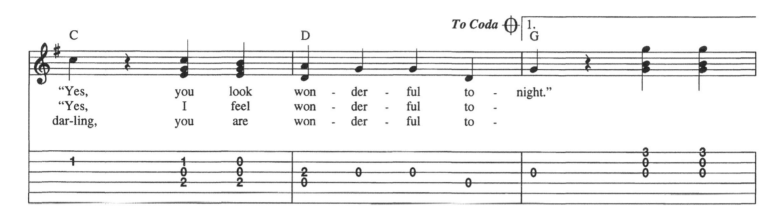

*To Coda* ⊕

"Yes, you look won - der - ful to - night."
"Yes, I feel won - der - ful to -
dar-ling, you are won - der - ful to -

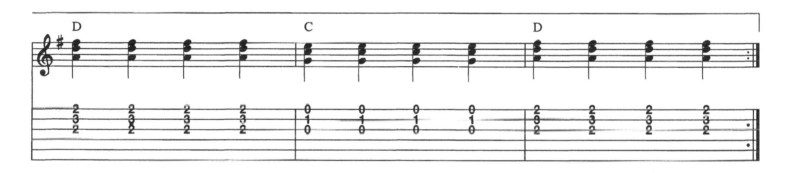

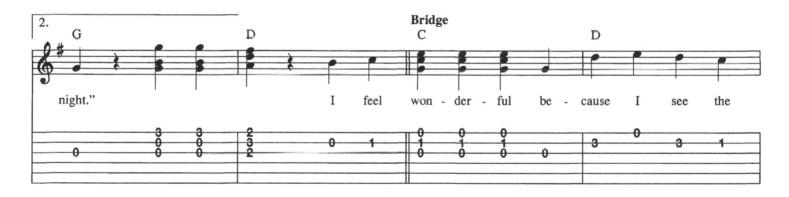

night." I feel won - der - ful be - cause I see the

love light in your eyes. Then the won - der of it all it that you

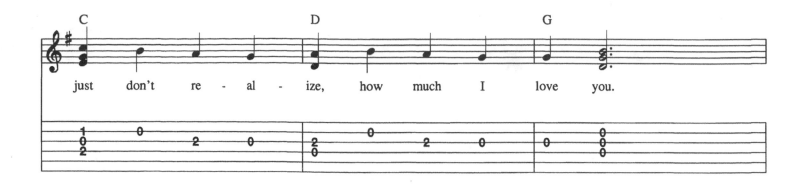

just don't re - al - ize, how much I love you.

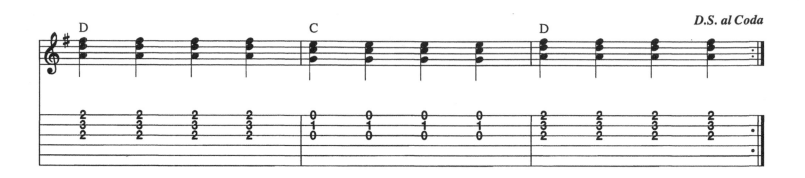

*D.S. al Coda*

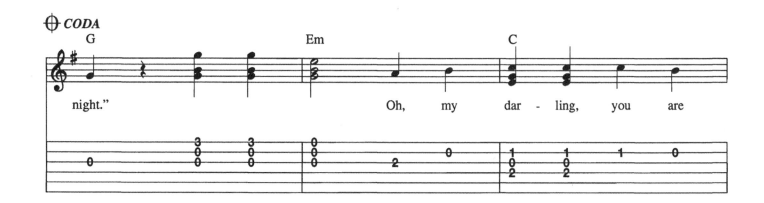

✦ *CODA*

night."  Oh, my  dar - ling, you  are

won - der - ful  to - night.

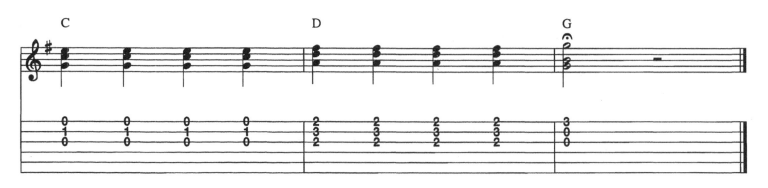